MO FANNING

Talking out loud

Sparkling tips for writing great dialogue

SPRING STREET BOOKS

First published in Great Britain by Spring Street Books in 2018

This version published in Great Britain in 2020

Copyright © 2020 by Mo Fanning

All rights reserved. No part of this publication may be reproduced, stored or transmitted in any form or by any means, electronic, mechanical, photocopying, recording, scanning, or otherwise without written permission from the publisher. It is illegal to copy this book, post it to a website, or distribute it by any other means without permission.

Mo Fanning asserts the moral right to be identified as the author of this work.

Mo Fanning has no responsibility for the persistence or accuracy of URLs for external or third-party Internet Websites referred to in this publication and does not guarantee that any content on such Websites is, or will remain, accurate or appropriate.

Second edition

ISBN: 978-0-9559885-6-1

Spring Street Books
Stourbridge, Great Britain

mofanning.co.uk

... 'and what is the use of a book,' thought Alice, 'without pictures or conversations?'

Lewis Carroll: Alice's Adventures in Wonderland

Contents

Everyone talks	1
In actual life	3
What's it for, anyway?	6
On and on and on	7
He said, she said	11
Who's doing the laundry?	15
Pump up the volume	19
Say it again?	21
Storytelling done bad	23
Everything sounds the same	25
We're characters in a sit-com	28
The Performance	30
Presentation is everything	32
Away you go	34
The Armchair Bride	35
Thanks for reading	46
About the Author	47
Also by Mo Fanning	48

Everyone talks

Readers love your characters to talk. Get this wrong and you'll lose your audience quicker than you can cram back story into mundane conversation.

Your readers care little about the art of creating a believable plot. They don't give a fig about whether your settings are correct. But they understand how actual people talk. They hear it every day. Most of them talk too. Given the garret mentality so many writers adopt, chances are readers are far better at conversation than those of us who claim to reorder words for a living.

Pick up any book and skim to dialogue.

The words sound natural, right?

A lot of work has gone into making sure they do!

If the writer has done their job, you won't notice how they steer each situation to move the plot forwards.

New writers either decide they hate dialogue and do everything in their power to avoid letting their characters talk, or they go to the other end of the spectrum and cram their stories with flabby exchanges. A talented writer realises the power of dialogue and uses it to both advance their story and build sympathetic characters.

Chances are, when you tell friends or colleagues that you're writing/have written a book, they glaze over and tell you how they've always wanted to do likewise. There's a book in everyone, after all - even if, in most cases, that book should remain lodged in the would-be author's pancreas.

People imagine they can write, because talented writers make it look easy.

A masterful story-teller makes everything appear simple, and I've designed this short guide to help all authors great and small master the basics.

I'll explain why dialogue matters (as much as the story), and why even the best, most sparkling scene you ever wrote might have to end up on the cutting room floor. It's key to creating believable characters.

I don't claim to be any better at creating realistic dialogue than the next person. As with any self-help book, take what you need and season my suggestions with a hefty shake of sceptical salt, but I can't recall a single critical review (I've had many) that slated my dialogue.

With that in mind, here's what I *think* I know about getting dialogue right.

In actual life

I will use this phrase **a lot**. So get used to it. It's my mission to correct any idea you might have that dialogue on the page should reflect the conversations you have or hear every day. When I first wrote, I was sure of one thing. My characters would speak just like the people around me. They'd um, err and repeat themselves. They'd talk nonsense and get things wrong.

> 'Hi,' Andy said.
> 'Hang on, I'm erm, just finishing off this email, I... yep, that's about it. Right,' Kieran looked up from his keyboard. 'What can I do you for, kind sir?'
> 'OK, so listen. Say no if you don't want to, but you know, I was just thinking, and God knows, I don't do that often enough, but, would you, err, like to look after the new girl?'
> 'Oh, erm, right, yeah, well, urm, sure, yeah, but, erm? Well, I'm not sure I'll have enough time, like because this report is kinda urgent, but you know...'

Soon enough I learned that if the written world sounds like a conversation, I might hear in the actual world, I'd got it wrong.

Writing dialogue isn't about reproducing actual life, it's about creating an impression of it-and let's be honest, making it better.

When you write a book, you cut the dull scenes. The same ruthless editor should take an axe to conversations between your characters. Work out what matters and what moves the story on. Show conflict (or collusion) and boil down your dialogue.

When you read a review praising the author for their grasp of 'natural dialogue', one thing's for sure, they worked hard to create the effect.

When I fancied myself as a stand-up comic, I took a course. Live comedy has a language of its own. A rhythm that tells the audience to expect a punchline to follow your set-up. One tip offered by the otherwise objectionable teacher was to write only five words before you place a full stop. Short sentences work in that environment. Often this is how we talk. But beware. Variety of sentence length matters. Fill your book with short sharp sentences and the reader soon grows tired.

Real-life dialogue - as I hope I showed above - can become unreadable. Journalists know this. They have it in their power to make their interviewees look dumb by printing what they say word-for-word. And while an unpleasant interviewee might tempt them into a hatchet job, they know this approach rarely makes for sparkling copy. Or repeat bookings from the editor.

As writers, we want our characters to carry the story; they need to come over as real. But actual people are weird. They don't always talk about important things. They pass comment on the weather or tell you what they binge watched last night on Netflix. And unless you're writing a niche story, this isn't what your readers want.

And then there's the long rambling set piece.

Yes, it lets you show off. Yes, you've seen plays or films (or even read books) where someone makes a stirring speech that changes everything. But it risks slowing things down. Not that this is a bad thing in every case. Maybe you *want* to give the reader pause for thought. The sad fact is, more often than not, they'll see a page of close-typed dialogue and skip ahead.

It works in a film or play because there's visual distraction. On the printed page, unless handled right, it's just words.

People don't deliver long soliloquies in everyday situations. Unless they're unhinged.

Bob walked into the office.

'Good morning all,' he said. 'I had a pig of a journey this morning. The bus was late and then when it came there were no free seats. I stood all the way. And because there was a broken down truck in the bus stop, they dropped us halfway up the street. There was a queue at the coffee shop and they were training an unfamiliar girl, so she got my order wrong and I've had to suffer the indignity of a cappuccino when everyone knows I'm more of a flat white kind of guy. How is everyone, good I trust? Did we all have a pleasant evening?'

If you want to write a long speech, create a reason. Perhaps a character has picked up an award, is retiring, telling a story or when they are giving a speech at a conference.

You might still want to break up the words with observations of what's going on around, or some inner monologue.

As a writer, you don't have the film-maker luxury of a camera to pan across faces.

What's it for, anyway?

I'm not about to suggest that you scrutinise every single exchange in your story against set criteria... but if I did, this would be what to consider:

- **Does the dialogue move the story forward?** Look at each chunk of dialogue and see if you've advanced the story and moved closer to the next peak or trough. You need to pull the reader along, ever closer to the climax of the story. *How's the weather?* rarely moves the plot -unless a tremendous storm is brewing, and that is behind whatever happens next.
- **Do your words reveal (relevant) information about the character?** Obviously not every exchange will explore a new, previously untold depth to the people on your pages, but they need to be consistent with what happened previously, or confirm their personality by how they react to words fired their way. Quality dialogue brings insight into how a character feels, and their motivations.
- **Are you making clear how characters relate?** The way characters talk to each other should help peg their place in a social circle. They might adjust how they speak when dealing with officials (either up or down, depending on their outlook on life).

On and on and on

This is the title of an awful filler track on one of Abba's *golden period* albums. It should serve as a warning to us all. Even the best can do the worst.

Some authors can get away with rambling dialogue. Joyce allowed Molly Bloom to witter on without constraint. Robertson Davies - I'm reliably informed - wrote a whole trilogy between quotation marks.

Does that mean it's right?

I'm firmly of the opinion it's as rude in fiction as in actual life (see, I said I'd keep using this phrase) to dominate the conversation.

> 'Something's bothering me,' Angie said. 'Don Foster might well like us to think he's innocent, and that's just why he's acting like that. And you never know he might well not think he is guilty of anything. Perhaps he thinks what he did was perfectly normal, and that everyone does stuff like that. Well, newsflash. they don't. But don't you think it's weird how he called round to see his elderly aunt Sally the night before we found her dead? And from that note she left, he lied to her. It's like he's been lying to everyone. If you ask me, we should tell the police.'

Dialogue that goes on for too long becomes like a tennis match, with the reader switching between characters. Following on from what I said at the end of the last chapter, as a general rule, if your characters talk for more than a handful of lines on the page, they've gone too far. You probably need to split things up.

Add dialogue tags (more later), a small shard of activity. Some glorious inner monologue where you get to explore true motivation, doubt, or even bare-faced arrogance.

Another way to dispose of a long and inelegant speech is to cut it entirely, paraphrase it (maybe more inner monologue) and top-and-tail the passage with actual dialogue.

'Something's bothering me,' Angie said.

Don Foster may well claim innocence. For all she knew, he may even think himself without blame. But was it mere coincidence he called on his aunt the evening before she turned up dead? A dreadful thought took hold. If he'd lied to her, he'd lied to everyone.

'We should tell the police.'

Another reason to trim long speeches is that readers like variety. Varying line length matters. If everyone speaks in similar-sized chunks, it can get dull. You lose that other vital quality: pace.

'I wonder if we should go to the scene of the crime again?' Julia said.
'What good would that do? We went over everything last time?'
'I can't help but think we may have missed something important.'
'We were thorough. Have you seen how many notes I took?'
'Yes, but all the same. Would another visit hurt anything?'
'I suppose not. Do you want to go now or shall we have a cup of tea first?'

It's dialogue for sure. The story (kind of) advances, but it hardly sets the page on fire. And the conflict between Julia and her colleague is dreadfully mild. I'd even suggest their voices sound too similar. I'll return to this later.

By varying line length, you create unique speech patterns and alter the rhythm.

'I wonder if we should go back to the crime scene?' Julia said.

> *Chris looked up from his notes. 'Why?'*
> *'I can't help but think we may have missed something.'*
> *'Have you even seen the notes I took?'*
> *'Would another visit hurt?'*
> *'Fine,' he said and dropped what remained of his sandwich into the bin,* *'get your coat.'*

While I'm on the subject, short bursts of dialogue can also ruin the pace of a scene. They speed things up - and if you take this too far, your characters risk coming over like cartoons.

> *'What's wrong?'*
> *'Nothing.'*
> *'Nothing?'*
> *'I said, didn't I?'*
> *'So nothings' wrong?'*
> *'No.'*
> *'You're sure?'*
> *'Yes.'*
> *'Fine.'*
> *'Fine.'*

I'm sure we've all had similar terse conversations with a loved one, it need not make it to our story. Remember what I said about being better than actual life? The quick-fire dialogue above adds little to a story and could easily frustrate the reader. The pace picks up, but the story slows right down. It's all conflict. And there's a distinct lack of dialogue tags - more of which in the next chapter.

> *'What's wrong?' I said, and Mike smiled.*
> *'Nothing.'*
> *'Really? because you're acting like it's something.'*
> *'There's nothing wrong.'*

TALKING OUT LOUD

'So why does it feel like there's something you don't want me to know?'
'Leave it.'
He gets up to go, but I block his way.
'You might as well tell me. I'll find out, anyway.'

He said, she said

*"To write adverbs is human, to write **he said** or **she said** is divine."*
Stephen King

Beginner writers **hate** this rule. They rail against it in every way they can. I was once such a writer. *How can 'said' be right every time?* I argued. *Why can't my characters rant, shout, whimper or mewl?*

And then, I saw that professional writers almost always avoid words other than *say* or *said*. That's because (scientific research apparently proves) the reader gets blind to them. Their reading brains skip over the words *say* or *said, and* stay in the action.

Say and *said* are the nuts and bolts of writing. They work like punctuation. The reader knows they're there, but they carry little meaning.

In most cases, it should be fairly obvious which character is talking - especially where the scene is a conversation between two people. However, when you add a third, you must tag things every few lines. Think back to things you've read. It's tiresome to have to stop and retrace the conversation to make sure you're on top of who said what.

If you find a scene between many characters getting untidy, another way to break things up is to add movement, internal dialogue, gestures, and expressions instead of tags.

'How can I make it up to you?' Evie said.
'Make your apology sound real.'

The suggestion came from a woman in green, sat near the door.
Evie stared.
'It is real.'
'Doesn't sound it.'
And then the chants began.
'Fraud, fraud, fraud.'
They hate me, she thought. They really hate me.

'Get her off the stage,' the man in black said. 'She's wasting our time.'
On the whole, you want it to absorb your reader in the story. They shouldn't feel like they're reading something that someone else has made up. The written word shouldn't feel written. The author should never really intrude.

Perhaps you decide it comes across as dull to keep writing *say* or *said*. It's easy to give in to temptation and sex things up.

Well guess what, you can. If you get bored with 'said', there's always 'asked'.

You can bend the rule further, now and then. Do it too often and you might as well stamp *amateur* on the cover of your book.

'You're right,' he thundered.
'I am,' she chuckled uproariously. 'I always am.'
'But how did you know?' he whined.
'Women's instinct,' she chirped.
'Will I ever understand you,' he groaned.
'Not if I have my way,' she whispered quietly.

Apart from the fact you don't need a 'tag' after every line of dialogue, you should also be able to find better ways to convey emotion in your words.

'Damn it, you're right,' he said.
'I always am.'
'But how did you know?'
'Women's instinct.'
He sat back in his chair, eyes closed. 'Will I ever understand you?'

She leaned in to whisper. 'Not if I have my way.'

Of course, you don't need to keep using 'he said' or 'she said' in every line. That gets old fast and takes the reader too far from the story. It should be obvious who is talking from how you set a scene or the style of language used. You can also add action after words to convey who spoke:

'You think so?'
'It's an option.' Jerry reached for his drink. 'Don't you agree?'

Before I stop talking tags, permit me a ride on my hobby horse. It's not possible to smile, snort or huff your words. If you do it. **Stop**. That's not to say a character can't smile, snort or huff, but these are **not** valid dialogue tags.

'Dinner is for wimps,' he huffed.

Is an obvious example of evil at work in the mind of some writer.

'Dinner is for wimps,' he said with a huff.

Is better, but I'm still worried that anyone thinks that about dinner. Because they matter so much, I'll return to tags in Chapter Six.

Adverbs

There are many writers who insist you edit out *every* adverb, but I suggest they have an occasional place. They serve a writer well when the words spoken are at odds with what they feel.

'I had the most wonderful time last night,' she said sadly.

On the whole, though, it's your job as a writer to set up the context for the emotion the adverb wants to convey.

'I'll leave,' she said sadly.

is a copout. Think of how you can better set this up. The lines you write before this snippet of dialogue before should give context, but a tiny action delivered with the words will help.

A tear rolled down her cheek. Her eyes met his.
'I'll leave.'

If you can't find a better way to convey the tone in someone's voice, break the show don't tell rule for once.

'I hate you,' he said bitterly

is weak.

'I hate you,' he said, with bitterness in his voice.

is better, but ideally, the writer will have set things up in advance and this relationship curve should come as no surprise.

Any chapter on adverbs would be incomplete without quoting the classics. The ones they throw at you in every creative writing class. See if you can spot what's wrong.

'Kiss me,' she whispered softly.
'Go away,' he shouted loudly.
'I hate everything about my life,' he thundered darkly.

Who's doing the laundry?

'**Laundry lists**' refer to writing where the author has tried to ram in as much detail as possible. Often because someone told them they needed to add 'more description or setting'. You see it most when a new character wanders onto the page:

> 'I was surprised by how she looked. Ellie is tall, tanned, slim and very, very blonde with big blue unblinking eyes that peer into your soul. She has such perfect skin and an obvious love of boho chic. When we met, she'd paired grey UGG boots with black shiny dance tights and added a pink ruffle skirt, topped off with a graphic print shirt. The overall look was of someone who got dressed in the dark. I found her voice raspy like someone who smoked many cigarettes, and she breathed heavily.'

Worse, it's deployed when setting up a scene in a new location:

> 'As you know, Robert, the cafe has always been dark and unwelcoming, the windows smeared with fingerprints. The rickety tables had seen better days. None of the chairs matched, and the floor was scuffed. Dog-eared menus sat between grubby salt and pepper shakers, and the air was thick with the smell of greasy bacon. The counter itself was littered with yesterday's free newspapers and in need of a good clean. A coat stand in the corner was overloaded with jackets. Red, blue, green, black and grey…'

If one character already knows, then why is the other character repeating it? In both cases, the reader is likely to lose interest fast, be overwhelmed, and most likely have the writer pegged for a rank amateur.

When you talk to your friends, you don't laundry list. You don't take a deep breath and deliver a blow-by-blow account of the day you've had. Unless you're in an absolute fouler of a mood, then you might.

And so it should be in your writing.

But first, let's get one thing clear. Writing authentic dialogue isn't the same as being able to scribe word for word what actual people say. You'll get no credit for jotting down that interesting conversation you overheard on the bus into town.

Real life dialogue is peppered with conversational ticks or *small talk*. And they should never make it into your story.

> 'Hello,' she said, as Monica sat.
> 'Hello.'
> 'How are you?'
> 'Fine, thanks, you?'
> 'Great.'
> 'Fabulous, right, so shall we get started?'
> 'Yes, please.'
> 'Great, so let me right to the point. How you have the nerve to show your face around here after what you did to Mary is beyond me.'

Start with the action:

Monica sat. She looked up. 'How you have the nerve to show your face around here after what you did to Mary is beyond me.'

And what if you have a bunch of stuff you want to tease out in conversation? Again, the written word needs to work differently to the actual world. In a story, dialogue should move the story on, create *or* confirm conflict, keep the reader engaged. Monica and her friend's greetings tell us nothing, move the story nowhere and as pleasant as it all may sound, you'll tune out fast.

How about if things took a different turn?

> Monica sat. Katie nodded hello. 'How are you?' she said.
> The obvious answer would be that Katie felt awful. She hadn't slept. She'd dreaded this meeting. But the truth wasn't an option.
> 'Fine,' she said.
> Monica shuffled papers. 'Shall we get started?'

By adding in some action, a smidge of inner monologue and suggesting what lies beneath, there's a story to be told.

Tuning out the ramble

In actual life, when you talk to people, they're more likely to respond to the first thing you say than the last. People latch onto initial words (or arguments) and prepare their answers. They tune out the rest of the ramble. It's human nature.

In fiction again, things work differently. Like I said above, dialogue exists to carry your story. And the writing needs to reflect that.

The average reader carries the last words they've read into the next sentence, so rearrange the words spoken to allow each character to respond to the last line delivered.

That's not to say you can't have a character machine-gun ideas:

> 'We need to clean the kitchen. Mum will be furious if she finds it like this. And the bedroom. One of us should make the beds and fluff up pillows. You know how fussy she gets about that. And have you seen the bathroom? It's like a bomb went off. She will go ape when she sees the dining room. Who let the dog in there, anyway?'
> 'Dude,' I said. 'Slow down. One thing at a time.'

Writing with a purpose

Did I mention already that dialogue should always help move your story along? I did, because it's the golden rule.

It's a way to add depth to your characters and convey information. When your writing reaches the editing stage, ask yourself if a conversation adds anything. Would the story stand without it?

> 'I saw Glenda at the beach,' Tilly said.
> 'Really?'
> 'Yes, she was walking her dog.'
> 'I didn't know she had a dog.'
> 'Yes, it's a golden retriever.'
> 'Fancy.'

Unless Glenda's dog will play a vital role in a later scene, this sparkling exchange might need to go.

Pump up the volume

As I've already said (at length) in Chapter 4, the temptation exists to have a character do something other than *say* their words. Remember how I said it's OK to bend the rules now and then?

It is.

But - in the words of the late George Michael - *if you're going to do it, do it right*.

Think before you write.

Does your chosen rule-breaking tag work in context?

So many people use *hiss* when their sentence has not a single *ss* sound.

'You ought to get changed,' he hissed.

And then there are those who will have characters *spit* their words with no good reason.

'You might have explained,' she spat.

And worse, an otherwise perfectly articulate character might mutter when clarity is of the essence.

'It's third right at the North Circular turn off and follow the road six blocks before you hang a left,' he muttered. 'If we don't make the hospital in time, I may never see my father alive again.'

And what about characters that resort to whispers when all around is chaos? It annoys the heck out of me when characters do it in TV soaps, more so in a novel.

> The wall gave way and chunks of concrete hit the ground, and Josh turned to his friend.
> 'We have to escape,' he whispered.

These are fairly obvious faults, but the worst is when you do things that can't work. Much like someone whispers as a building falls around them - or when plotting murder in the Queen Vic.

Another place you can't get away with whispering is on board a plane. If you don't believe me, try it. It can't be done. There's too much ambient noise.

Ever tried to share a secret in a crowded bar? Even with hands cupped to ears, there's a damn good chance someone will mishear. That could be intentional…

> 'We have to go,' she whispered.
> He didn't hear and waved down the barman.
> 'Same again?'
> And that's how we ended up in that bed once more. Every good intention forgotten. I made a note that from that day forward, I would only split up with boyfriends in the safety of a public library.

And then there's the **sigh**.

Has *anyone* ever truly been able to sigh a sentence… and have anyone understand their words? Go on. Try. I'll wait.

Limp prose uses this trope *all the time*. Fair enough, now and then a character might say something with a sigh, but limit exposure.

Before you know it, your dialogue ends up like happy hour at the chest clinic.

Say it again?

There is good repetition and bad repetition. Repetition can work. But let's look first at what happens when bad writing happens to good people.

In actual life, we repeat ourselves all the time. On the page, it doesn't always work.

> 'I don't know... I don't know... I just don't... I don't,' he said.
> Charlie stared at Martin. Why did he sound like a stuck record?

You can get away with repetition occasionally, but keep doing it, and it slows down the pace. It's all very well for an author to insist that this is how people talk, but look back at what I told you in Chapter 2. Your writing needs to improve on actual life.

> His head in his hands, he muttered to himself.
> 'I don't know.'
> Over and over.
> Charlie could do nothing but wait.

Repetition is a great tool to help characters come to terms with something awful. You'll sometimes want to ask characters to doubt they've heard an uncomfortable truth. They may ask someone to repeat themselves, but that doesn't mean whoever spoke first saying it all again.

> 'I heard him on the phone to her. I was hanging out the washing. It

was Tuesday. They were discussing a holiday.'
'What?'
'I said I heard him talking to her on the phone. I was hanging out the washing. It was Tuesday. They were discussing a holiday.'

It's slow and lazy. Inauthentic. And rubbish. Also, it makes your writing hard to read as the pace drains away.

How about this:

'I heard him on the phone to her. They were discussing a holiday.'
'What?'
'You heard me.'

Sometimes a repeated word or phrase hammers home a point. Just don't overdo it. Because repetition stands out, it has power. And that power can turn readers off.

At the top of this chapter, I promised you that there is such a thing as good repetition. Well-chosen words and phrases can emphasise what you want to get into the head of your reader.

'**I warned you** this would happen, **I warned you**, and **you** refused to listen. **I warned you** and now look. Someone died here. Help me move the body.'

Used well, it can improve dialogue and lend rhythm to speech patterns. It can emphasise the character. The reader tunes in without noticing. In the snippet above, I pictured someone obsessive or frustrated, and maybe a little supportive.

Storytelling done bad

Inexperienced writers rely on dialogue to deliver the story. It's an absolute no-no. Victoria Wood satirised this best in her mock soap 'Acorn Antiques':

"Apparently, being spiteful and having lots of extra-marital affairs could bring back my jaundice, so I'm going to be really nice from now on."

The fancy word for this is 'exposition'. Dialogue that exists supposedly to benefit the reader.

'John's dead,' she said.
 'John, our grandfather? The man who brought us up single-handed after our parents died in that terrible plane crash? That John?'

There's no reason your dialogue can't help to set up the character of whoever it is who's speaking, but when they're filling in the reader, it doesn't work.

'I blame it on my upbringing. If my father hadn't been abandoned by his mother at the age of six so she could go on a round the world cruise, I can't help thinking things would have been very different,' she said.

The temptation to do this comes from another age-old writing rule: SHOW, DON'T TELL. Inexperienced writers imagine that by showing someone talking, they're not telling. They're wrong. Think about when you've been trapped by the pub bore, and as they tell their latest story, you struggle to care. They often acknowledge your lack of interest with a zinger like 'You had to be there'.

Ask yourself if anyone would deliver the lines you wrote. Are they saying what they're saying because you wanted to TELL the reader something about the story.

Although, sometimes you need to have a character recount the plot. Police procedurals are rife with that sort of thing, but even then, a talented writer trims the fat.

When characters first meet, they know nothing of each other. Unless you've set it up (which you could well do), the first time they talk, there's no back story. They only know of their immediate situation.

As the scene unfolds, you can tease out a story, but trust your reader to pick up things you leave unsaid. You can add in story around the spoken word. Often you don't need your characters to know everything about each other or the situation, but the reader may get an insider view.

'I blame it on my upbringing,' she said.

When he didn't react, she explained how her parents split. How her father struggled to bring her up when her mother booked herself on a round the world cruise.

The rules

- **DON'T** have characters tell each other things they should already know, never let them remind each other about things that happened in the past, just so the reader *gets* it.
- **DON'T** have characters explain everything in horrible detail.
- **DON'T** have characters tell each other how it makes them feel - or worse, why (especially if it's because of that awful thing in their past).

Everything sounds the same

The worst sin of all (in writing obviously, there are other sins in other professions that rank way higher) is to write dialogue that makes all your characters sound alike.

It's an obvious pitfall. After all, each character came from your single twisted mind. Even if you base them on people you know, love or hate, they'll reflect you.

You need every being in your story to come over as unique.

You've probably already put in the time describing your characters and making them distinct, so why throw everything away with bland generic dialogue?

Every character you write should think and act in their own ways.

The words you give them to say should reflect this uniqueness.

Think first about the character sketches you have in your head, or - if you're a super-organised planning kind of writer - in your copious notes. You already know what makes the people on the page tick, so whatever they say needs to fit with that.

- A grieving widow probably won't chip in witty punch lines. The office joker might.
- Compare a gruff *'yeah'* with a considered *'I see what you mean.'*
- The morose caretaker - who the reader will later find out killed everyone - won't speak like a Valley Girl.

Much as I mildly mock writers who *over-plan*, it's vital to understand your characters. Not knowing them inside out is the most frequent cause of writer's block.

Time spent in advance working out their backgrounds is time well spent. And it naturally should influence how they talk.

I apologise for what follows. It's a terrible example of sweeping generalisations, but...

- An Oxford Don will have a wider vocabulary (unless he's a total fraud).
- A guy who digs the road might swear more (or not, that might make him interesting).
- A poet might speak in more ethereal terms.
- The morose caretaker might be prone to quoting Chaucer (I'm obsessed, let me have this one).

It's perfectly acceptable to allow the spoken word to contain poor grammar or the wrong choice of words. But don't go mad with it. Affectation can spoil an otherwise splendid story.

If a character swears, don't have them do it every second word - unless you're Irvine Welsh.

If your characters are children, are they speaking like children, or are they delivering long sentences littered with long words?

Just as when you want to convey a regional or foreign accent, don't turn your writing into a pastiche of BBC 'sitcom' "Allo Allo".

> *"I was pissing by the door, when I heard two shits. You are holding in your hand a smoking goon; you are clearly the guilty potty."*

In actual life, we alter how to speak depending on who we are talking to and this should happen in your writing too.

A teacher in an inner city school might talk to her colleagues differently to the parents who come to discuss their kid's progress. And what happens when they're away from the confines of school, could suggest they're a different person in different settings.

Writers sometimes use non-verbal ticks to define their characters. This is another thing to use with care.

Having the elderly professor clear her throat in every scene, mutter or mumble, fart or sit in lumbering silence gets old fast.

These are ticks best saved for minor characters.

In the world of sitcom writing, *Friends* is often cited as a touchstone. Each character has a unique way of talking. If you read a script with the character names redacted, you would know exactly who says which lines. Think about *your* friends. They don't all sound the same. We adapt the way we speak depending on who we're with.

When your characters speak, they should stay true to who they are. Even without character tags, the reader should know who spoke.

We're characters in a sit-com

It's fair enough to have characters deliver witty lines - especially if you're writing a rom-com. But think about it. How many people do you know who can quick-fire joke after joke? Witty observation after witty observation?

This is the job of the stand-up comedian. Someone who will have toiled for days, weeks, months and years over their material. They're working from a script.

And they do occasionally get tempted into writing books, but again, they often rehash their stand-up act, unless they're taking the novel writing thing seriously.

I've heard it said, you can't teach someone to be funny, and yet I've never met anyone who doesn't understand what is or isn't funny. For most of us, if we receive a witty text, we'll find a way to reply in the same way. This is comic dialogue, albeit in its simplest form.

The aim of this book is to offer hints on how to write authentic dialogue. The odd joke is fine. Too many, and you've over-egged the pudding.

> 'Hi,' Mike said. 'You look like I feel.'
> 'What's that supposed to mean?'
> 'Like someone who will get punched if he answers that question.'
> 'No seriously, what do I look like?'
> 'Like a dude who keeps asking tough questions.'
> 'My dog's got no nose.'
> 'How does it smell?'
> 'Awful.'

You might think you're being clever with your brilliant joke, (and you most likely are) but is that *you* speaking or the character? And if it is the character, are you handing them a burden? Are they obliged to keep quick-firing jokes?

Mike - in the above example - appears like someone with a ready answer to every question. But how tiring will that become? Will the reader ever get under his skin? Will he ever form a relationship with other characters?

Or maybe that's something to explore - Mike's darker side. How he acts when the spotlight is off.

If you are aiming to inject humour into your dialogue, remember that what one person finds funny, others find annoying.

Think long and hard about whether the humour should come from the dialogue or elsewhere.

Comedy comes from situations rather than from words and trying to shoehorn jokes into what your characters say is often a recipe for disaster.

My books sit firmly in the category of romantic comedy, but that doesn't mean I sit in my writing room and chortle the day long. Inspiration often fails to strike. In those cases, I write a chapter straight - with no comedy. This gets the plot sorted. I then go back over the words and 'funny it up'.

A writer must create an image in the reader's mind that makes them smile.

It doesn't matter if you don't think of yourself as a brilliant comedian - Shakespeare wrote comedy, but from all reports was a miserable sod at parties. What matters is that you create characters and situations that make the reader laugh.

Your characters need to play off against each other, interact, and manipulate situations to produce the humour. We do not base funny dialogue on one-liners.

The Performance

Every book, blog or *cheat sheet* will tell you the same. The best way to check your dialogue *works* is to read it out loud.

Most every time I sit back and smugly tell myself that I nailed that scene, my opinion changes when I lock myself away and *perform* said conversation.

The performance - as I so grandly call it - is where you bring everything together. All the tips and advice I've offered in this book count for nothing if you don't road test the final product before you send it on its way into the world.

It's dialogue. Conversation. Words spoken out loud. It should sound natural and flow easily. And be prepared for a shock. Often what flows in our minds doesn't sound so great out loud.

The performance is also a great way to get free proof reading. The awkward phrases that your brain misses as you stare at the screen or page gets caught by your tongue.

All those typos, awkward sentences and words you've used *way* too many times jump out. If things don't sound right, change the order or swap out words.

Have you used the right amount of tags - or too many? Have you allowed yourself one too many adverbs? Is the emotion clear, or have you fallen back on filling in the blanks? Is there room between lines for narrative or brief description and action? Or have you done this way too many times, resulting in something long and hard to enjoy?

'Joe,' she said as she reached for his hand. 'You know I love you.'

THE PERFORMANCE

Joe didn't look up, his eyes stayed fixed on the scene playing out across the room.

'She thinks we're getting married,' he said, and sniffed hard.

Mary wanted him to look at her, and so shifted her chair, until in his eyeline.

'Why are you doing this?' she said, as a tear rolled down her cheek.

Joe brushed it away with his finger.

'It isn't what I want,' he said and closed her eyes.

She shook her head. 'Nor me, so let's run away.'

Joe imagined how Mary ever thought this a viable plan. But he loved her too.

'OK,' he said with the broadest of smiles. 'It's a deal'.

Just like with the earlier example I gave about the sitcom 'Friends', you should be able to look at any part of your story and know which character is speaking, simply by reading their words. Each character needs his or her own voice.

And before I get into technical matters, I want to quote Aaron Bennett:

Rewriting is essential. Especially when it comes to dialogue. There is always a better line, a better set-up, a better pay-off.

Presentation is everything

So that's about it in terms of how to create authentic dialogue. There's a hundred more books out there that will add to the basics, but I hope it's been a blast.

At some point, you'll want to share what you've written with others. You might choose to self-publish, or approach an agent or publisher. Or enter your story into a competition.

It could be the best story ever, with dialogue that sings, but if you get the presentation wrong, you've lost the battle. What follows are tips on how to format dialogue in any book or manuscript.

Quotation marks

First up, the age-old question. Single or double?

The answer - as you might expect - is an unsatisfying *it depends*.

In the UK, there has been a move in recent years to single quote marks around dialogue. In the US, the preference is for double.

You may find both in use. In my books, I write with single quote marks, but rely on double marks when referring to a title.

'Evie knew about it,' Guido said.
   'How could she?'
   He reached for his copy of "The Great Book of Facts" and found the page.
   'This is her handwriting, isn't it?'

Punctuation

When the dialogue tag forms part of a sentence, use a punctuation mark after the speech, close the quote marks, and use a lowercase letter for the tag.

> The house was a mess.
> 'How can I be expected to keep things tidy with three lads bouncing round the place?' he said.
> Mary slumped into a chair.

Even though this example sees the speech end with a question mark, you still use a lowercase letter. It would be the same with an exclamation mark. This is because the tag is a part of the sentence. When there's no tag after the dialogue, use a full stop and close the quote marks.

> 'She started it,' he said
> 'No, I didn't.'
> And so, they reached a stalemate.

When dialogue continues after the tag, and is still a part of the same sentence, use a comma. The next part of dialogue then requires a lower-case letter.

> 'You broke it,' Mike said, 'and that means you can take the blame.'

If there's a break in the sentence, you end the tag with a full-stop and start the next sentence of dialogue with an uppercase letter.

> 'You broke it,' Mike said. 'I've just heard their car in the drive. Best get your excuses ready.'

Away you go

I'll end my sermon on speech with one final tip. Greetings and saying goodbye doesn't matter.

In your *actual life*, you almost always say hello and bid fond farewells, it's not needed in your novel. It comes back to the 'small talk' rules I suggested right at the start of our time together.

Set up a scene by describing how your characters enter or leave the room or conversation.

> *And with that Mo sits back in his chair, smiles at the screen and yawns.*
> *His work here is done.*

The Armchair Bride

I thought you might like a sneak peep at my first novel, published way back in 2008 and recently updated to mark ten years since I took my first steps into writing. It's available from bookstores and booksites everywhere.

Ten, nine, eight...

Does anyone love New Year's Eve? If I had my way, I'd be in bed with a good book and an enormous glass of wine. Not stuck to a threadbare carpet in a Manchester theatre function room and forced to pretend I want to spend the dying hours of the year with people I see every working day.

Seven, six...

A guy from the tech team grabs my hand and drags me to the dance-floor. He laughs in my face and tells me to *cheer up. It might never happen* and I play along, faking the most cheesy grin.

Might never happen? It already has.

Five, four, three...

We link arms, and anticipation grows. A new year, new hopes, new dreams. On the stroke of midnight, lives will change. All the bits about us we didn't like will vanish. We'll lose weight, stop smoking, stop drinking, join a gym, hug trees and life will be good.

Two... one...

The room erupts as Big Ben chimes and bagpipes quail. Streamers pop and party people hug, kiss and stumble.

Should old acquaintance be forgot and never brought to mind...

I mouth the first few words, air-kiss colleagues and do my absolute best to act like someone having oodles of fun. Across the room, my flatmate mine-sweeps abandoned glasses and necks leftover wine. My boss does his compulsory tour of duty to shake hands and exchange rousing words.

I've worked with Brian for nine years, and although it's never come up, I'm sure we're about the same age. Our cultural references tally and we share looks of dread when younger people use words like totes, bear or sick. He's good looking in a greying-at-the-temples football-dad way and keeps himself in shape. Brian dresses well and happens to have perfect teeth. Mam would call him *a decent catch*. My sisters would love him. The stumbler being, he's my boss. And married. To Audrey. Who everyone at the Empire Theatre fears.

Because she *is* terrifying.

'Am I getting a kiss?' I say when my turn comes. 'Or is this a handshake only deal?'

Brian looks around before leaning in to land the slightest peck.

'Happy new year, Lisa. Are you here with Andy?'

I nod and reheat my best fake smile. Obviously, I'm with Andy. I'm *always* with Andy. People tell running jokes about how we come as a pair.

Brian beams. 'Someone said you had a boyfriend, and I told them I'm *sure* you're still single.'

He means nothing by this, and would be mortified to know how much a throwaway comment hurts. Especially the word *still*.

I throw back my head and laugh.

'You know me, Brian. Young, free and unattached. Only not so much of the young. I'm all about girl power.'

I do the v-sign thing and pout like a perimenopausal Spice Girl.

'Right... so... that's good,' he says and takes a subtle step backwards. 'I best get back to Audrey.'

Ten minutes after midnight on New Year's Eve is the worst time ever to give yourself a *'where did things go wrong?'* pep talk. With my left foot jammed against a graffitied toilet door, I wish myself away. Twelve months ago - to the night - I was sure the upcoming twelve months would be my year. My lifestyle shopping list was small but perfectly formed: boyfriend, promotion, fit into (what I'm sure are wrongly labelled) jeans.

I'm still single, still doing the same job and, on Christmas Eve, found the inner strength to stuff those jeans in a bin bag of cast-offs and dump everything in the doorway of a cat rescue shop.

That's not to say I'm unhappy. Why would I be? Who needs a boyfriend when I share my life with Andy? We've been best mates for close on 20 years and long ago pledged to never become *sad normals*. Like anyone who's been around the block and feared for a lonely old age, we've drunk too much gin and agreed on a marriage pact. If single 40 ever rolls over to solo 60, we'll wave white flags and do what every other loser does. Fake a happy union to save on food costs and pool our winter fuel allowance. Until then, we're fine single.

People still talk about us as a pair.

Invite Andy and Lisa.

Will Andy and Lisa join us?

The flat-share thing renders us socially acceptable and allows us a taste of coupledom. Without the need to find reasons not to bother with sex. I still get to watch what I want on Netflix and don't have to pretend to like his boring mates or weird hobbies. Best of all, I get to inhale a Dairy Milk without guilt.

I date. Though treat it more like an extreme sport than something that might lead to wedded bliss. My brief encounters with suitable men come courtesy of blind dates engineered by well-meaning friends. I tried Tinder once. The evening ended with me seeking legal advice to slap a restraining order on a man called Tom who sent me daily tokens of his love. Locks of his ex-wife's hair, shards of her wedding dress, a photo of them together with my face superglued on hers.

And he proved to be one of my more successful dates.

New Year's Eve is when the nagging doubts grow loud. What if the *sad normals* are right?

Mam insists an old shoe exists for every old sock, and a quick search online throws up photos of the much better times that *everyone* from school looks to be having. Dinner parties in Farrow & Ball homes, designer-frocked cocktail receptions in chi-chi bars. The girls I assumed would end up in prison pose with a Subaru, labradoodle, and scrubbed-up children.

And here's me, in the staff loo, alone.

Mam is right to worry. I'm the middle child and each time I find myself ditched, she says the same thing:

'What did you do to scare this one off, Lisa? We were *all* convinced he'd be the one.'

By *all*, she means my two sisters, and their lovely husbands. She also means all of her neighbours, our priest, sixteen of her closest friends and anyone with time to listen in the post office. Mrs Gupta, who handles the QVC returns, considers it an *absolute scandal* I'm not yet spoken for. She suggested burning herbs and lighting special candles to turn everything around.

I've become a stranger's pet project.

'Lisa. Don't take this the wrong way, but if you want to come out of the cupboard, that's fine with all of us,' Mam said when I called to check she'd got my Christmas cards.

'I have no idea what you're talking about.'

'Your father loved Virginia Wade and that Claire Balding is always well turned out. I considered buying myself a pair of jodhpurs.'

The penny landed with a crash.

'I'm not gay, Mam.'

'You're in denial.'

'Andy is gay. I'm straight.'

'They can marry these days. There's gay boys and girls on Coronation Street. Not that things ended well for those two lasses. One of them almost chucked herself off the underwear factory roof, but the wedding itself was grand. I've always said you suit lemon.'

I changed the subject. Mam never means to sound like she froths at the mouth. I blame the Daily Mail and the fact that my sisters like to wind her up. She has my best interests at heart.

For years, she liked to send pages torn from local newspapers showing former classmates dressed in horrible frocks and posing with new husbands.

'If fat Leslie Walker can snare a chap, you can too, Lisa.'

I blame her for *'The Spreadsheet'*.

Through the magic of Excel, I keep track of *every* girl from school. Each wedding, birth, messy split and second marriage gets recorded. The spreadsheet makes for depressing reading. Each girl from class 5B at Erdington Comp is spoken for; except for me and my onetime bestie Helen. And of late, even she's been seeing someone. Her last email humble-bragged about a thrilling trip to a garden centre, so it's only a matter of time before the postman brings my *save the date* card.

An impatient party-goer hammers on the toilet door.

'Hurry, Lisa. There's a queue.'

Back in the land of pretending to enjoy the best time ever, Andy tracks me down.

'How much longer do we need to endure this hellhole?'

I'm about to suggest an escape plan when a booming voice calls my name and chills my heart.

'Audrey,' I say, and try not to act terrified. Brian's wife is far from my biggest fan. She blames me for the state he ended up in after a tequila-fuelled cast and crew party in July.

She isn't wrong.

'Have you seen my husband?' she says. 'Reliable sources suggest he was last spotted with you.'

'He kissed everyone,' I say too fast. 'Not just me.'

Her face turns to stone, and I turn to Andy for help.

'Fabulous party,' he says. 'How do you manage this year after year?'

Disarmed, she fans herself with podgy fingers. 'One does one's best.'

She doesn't see the scattered debris, the spent Prosecco corks, torn tatty streamers and paper plates of abandoned beige food.

'Shouldn't you mingle?' she says with a sniff. 'You're junior management. We pay for occasions like these to facilitate team bonding.'

Half an hour of forced smiles leaves my jaw numb. I need to find Andy and scarper. Except I suspect that's what he's already done. Most likely to some crowded gay bar to have a much better time.

Defeated, I seek a chair in the darkest corner. A place to hide until it's safe to leave without causing upset. Automatic impulse sends me back online to read friend updates. A soft-focus, high-filter gallery from a spiteful girl who made my young life hell. Like all the *sad normals*, Ginny Baker is having fun; grinning for the camera on the arm of some bloke at what looks like a Hollywood-themed party. Ginny doesn't know I stalk her. Her security settings are shot.

A text pings from Helen to wish me a happy new year, and I imagine her at a brilliant party, with brilliant friends, having a brilliant time.

I reply with a sad face selfie and tell her I'm at a theatre party.

She texts back *jel-jel* and I reply *LOL*.

We like to crack on we're down with the kids.

Over by the bar, Brian raises a glass, and mouths do you want a drink?

I hold my nose and pull a face. He laughs, but still heads over.

'I got you one anyway,' he says. 'They tell me after six you stop noticing how awful it is.'

'The wine or this party?'

He looks around, his eyes wide. 'Both.'

'Don't let Audrey hear you say that.'

'She's too busy sucking up to the trustees to care. Her mission is refurbish the Royal Box and score a plaque with her name on.'

'If that happens, where will I go to eat my lunch?'

'Where will *I* hide to do the crossword?'

He pulls out a chair, sits and catches sight of Ginny's photos on my phone. 'Friend of yours?'

'We went to school together.'

'She looks older.'

I treat him to a rare, genuine smile. 'Just for that I won't bug you for a wage rise in January.'

A girl from accounts stumbles past with a bunch of mistletoe. We fake earnest conversation until the coast is clear.

'Good move,' Brian says, and I laugh. When he dares to loosen up, he's brilliant company.

'How's your evening been?' I say.

'Totes sick.'

Audrey hovers near the DJ booth, arms folded, glaring in our direction.

'Don't turn around,' I say. 'We're getting the death stare.'

He doesn't move his lips as he speaks. 'Audrey?'

I nod.

'Fine,' he says and gets to his feet. 'I'll throw myself on her mercy and take one for the team.'

For such a nice guy, he lacks any hint of a spine.

I watch her jab him with a podgy finger and issue orders. He looks around helplessly. Poor guy.

I'm lost in another online loop when Andy appears.

'I've been searching for you,' I say.

'Get your coat. We're going to the Mineshaft.'

'That's men only.'

'Keep your head down, nobody will know the difference.'

'If it's all the same to you…'

He grabs my hand. Resistance is futile.

The drink hits as we step outside and I find myself frog-marched to a waiting taxi. The gum-chewing cab driver peers over his shoulder as I collapse in a heap on his back seat. 'Is your lady going to be sick?'

Outraged, I try to point out I'm not anybody's *lady*, but the words come out slurred, and Andy takes over.

'The contents of my lady's stomach will be the least of your problems if you don't get us to the Mineshaft within the next ten minutes.'

In slow-moving traffic, drunks hammer on the cab windows.

'Is this the fastest you can go?' Andy says.

'New Year's Eve, mate. You'd be quicker walking.'

'Just drive. Run them over if need be.' When he pokes a finger in my ribs, I squeal. 'Don't fall asleep on me, Lisa.'

'I'm done. I want to go home.'

The driver's eyes lock onto mine. 'Are you OK, miss? This lad's not bothering you?'

'Oh please,' Andy snaps. 'The last man that bothered her lost the use of an eye. Your concern is noted, but do what you're being paid to do and drive.'

'I'm fine,' I say. 'This is how we talk to each other.'

Andy's arm slips around my shoulder, and he pulls me close. 'That staff party *was* awful. Why can't straights ever get it right? We need to find better excuses next year.'

'Brian hated the party too.'

He nods, but says nothing.

'Audrey forced him to come.'

'Yeah, whatever...'

'He's OK, you know?'

Andy shifts in his seat to face me. 'If he's so fabulous, why don't you start an affair?'

My cheeks burn. 'Andy...'

He throws back his head and howls. 'Jesus, Lisa. Your face. I was taking the piss. If Audrey got wind of you lusting about dreamy Brian, she'd break both your legs with a lump hammer.'

We join a line of cars at red lights.

'This is insane,' he says. 'We'll do our resolutions now.'

Each year, Andy and I pledge something mad that we know will never happen just for the hell of it. It's become our thing. Twelve months back, I said I would pilot a plane and learn salsa. He pledged fluency in French.

'New rule this year, we choose for each other,' he says and I blink in confusion. 'Just make something up... like tell me to shag more than three men called Dave.'

'Do you *know* more than three men called Dave?'

'No, but that doesn't matter. Hurry. Tell me what my fabulous future holds.'

'I'm too drunk. Ask me in the morning.'

'It has to be tonight, or it won't count.'

'Fine.' I haul myself upright. 'You must... be famous by this time next year.'

Andy's lips purse. I've broken one of our friendship rules. We *never* mention his less-than-stellar acting career. In common with most people in the Empire Theatre box office, he dreams of a life on the stage. To date, he's been a community theatre caterpillar and played a guy with bad breath in a telly commercial that only aired on the Isle of Wight.

'Call your agent,' I say. 'Demand she put you up for more stuff. In fact, give me your phone. I'll call her.'

He slaps away my hand. 'That's not how show business works.'

'You're fantastic though,' I say. 'You can do this.'

Compliments always work with Andy.

'How are you defining famous?'

'You get to appear on *The One Show*.'

'I already did that gig.'

'Face in the crowd doesn't count. Full Matt Baker or nothing. Your turn, do me.'

I can tell from how his eyes narrow I won't like whatever vengeful idea has crossed his mind.

But it's New Year's Eve. Whatever we say will be forgotten in days.

'Right,' he says. 'You want to do this?'

'You started the game.'

'By this time next year, you need to find a husband.'

All at once, the fun is sucked away.

'That's not fair,' I whisper. 'Why not lose weight or stop eating leftovers from the bin?'

'Both would help make you more appealing to the opposite sex.'

'Find something else.'

'I'm serious, Lisa. You spend half your life telling me how everyone is married or paired off. Next year, it's your turn.'

Anger bubbles. Why is he even doing this? He knows how soon I bruise.

'Stop sulking,' he says. 'We'll hang around Strangeways on release day.'

'I *could* get a man, if I wanted one.'

He snorts and turns to gaze out of the window. 'Look at the state of that lass. She's trashed.'

'I could,' I persist. 'Maybe I enjoy being on my own.'

'Yeah, right. Whatever.'

'Fine,' I say. 'I accept your silly challenge. I will find myself a serious boyfriend.' Andy reaches for my hand, but I snatch it away. 'And call Beryl. Just for once let's do something with our lives.'

'Oh, come on, pumpkin,' he says. 'Don't let's fall out. Not tonight of all nights.'

Blood pumps in my ears, and my chest aches. I'm either having a heart attack or tasting genuine fear.

An idea forms. Before I can stamp it down, it takes hold.

'You're fired,' I say in my best Lord Sugar voice.

Andy cocks his head to one side. 'I'm what?'

'You heard me. I'm your manager, and you are now out of a job. Free to follow your dreams.'

'You can't fire me.'

'I just did.'

'On what grounds?'

'Insubordination.'

'Fuck off.'

'How about arguing with customers? What about that woman with the fur coat you threatened to napalm?'

'She had that coming. Fur's for fools.'

'Don't you see?' I say, warming to my subject. 'If you don't need to drag yourself into work each day, you'll get to focus on your calling.'

'My what?'

'Your calling. The roar of the crowd. The smell of the greasepaint.'

'Have you suffered a stroke?'

'You expect me to find a man. Surely *you* can find someone who'll recognise your talent. Go to Hollywood, hang around the studios. This is what you always said you wanted to do.'

'Hollywood?'

'London then. I'll pay your train fare.'

If Andy's having problems believing what he hears, he isn't the only one. Somehow, in this moment, my mad ideas feel right.

'I'm letting you go,' I say. 'Giving you the space to live your dream.'

'I'll report you to the union.'

'You've *always* hated working in the box office. You said yourself you'd leave if you could afford to. This is my gift to you. I've enough put by to cover your share of the rent for a month or two. Call it a sabbatical.'

'You're being ridiculous.'

I take hold of his hand. 'If acting doesn't work out, you can come back.'

We've reached the club. A queue of guys in leather chaps and gimp suits glare as Andy springs from the cab and jumps the line.

Our driver turns around.

'I'll marry you, love. What are you like with a chipper?'

I rummage in my bag for money.

'Do you have a business card? And keep every Saturday free next December. I might be in touch.'

Thanks for reading

I'm busy working on a new novel for release in 2021. It's about what happens when a perfect life reduces to rubble. For Evie Fox, it might be the start of something big.

If you'd like to know more - and get advance chapters - please sign up to my mailing list through my website. I promise not to spam you daily with my insanity - if you want that sort of stuff, follow me on Twitter.

If you're looking for more of the writing tips stuff, try '**Please find attached**' - a guide to getting your writing in front of agents and publishers.

Sign up for my mailing list online at www.mofanning.co.uk

About the Author

Born in the Midlands, and living in Brighton via Amsterdam, occasional stand-up comic Mo Fanning's first book - **The Armchair Bride** - was shortlisted for the Arts Council Book of the Year in 2012.

After two collections of short stories - **This is (not) America** and the festive-themed **Five Gold Rings** - and a spell writing for BBC America and The Guardian, Mo is back. **Rebuilding Alexandra Small** is due in 2021.

If you'd like to know more - and get advance chapters - please sign up to Mo's mailing list.

You can connect with me on:
- http://mofanning.co.uk
- https://twitter.com/mofanning
- https://www.facebook.com/mofanningbooks

Subscribe to my newsletter:
- https://mofanning.co.uk/mailing-list

Also by Mo Fanning

The Armchair Bride
Barney finds money with strings attached. Anna longs for Ben - and cake, but can she have both? Martin gets what he didn't know he wanted, and a mother waits for a son who might never come home. Mo Fanning writes stories to make readers smile. And think. Comedy with a dark edge and characters you'll want to get to know. If you take nothing else from this fine collection of writing, you'll learn how to get stubborn stains out of white sofas.

Available in paperback and ebook

This is (not) America
Barney finds money with strings attached. Anna longs for Ben - and cake, but can she have both? Martin gets what he didn't know he wanted, and a mother waits for a son who might never come home. Mo Fanning writes stories to make readers smile. And think. Comedy with a dark edge and characters you'll want to get to know. If you take nothing else from this fine collection of writing, you'll learn how to get stubborn stains out of white sofas.

Available in paperback and ebook

**Five gold rings
Disarmingly dark when you least expect it**

Short stories to warm your heart at the coldest time of the year. From the stress of keeping up with the Denby-Smyths to full-on hostilities (briefly) set aside, Mo gives you his very special look at Christmas.

There's even one story suitable for the kiddies. Sort of.

Available in paperback and ebook

www.ingramcontent.com/pod-product-compliance
Lightning Source LLC
Chambersburg PA
CBHW032052290426
44110CB00012B/1057